A Puerto Rican Childhood

THIS EDITION

Editorial Management by Oriel Square
Produced for DK by WonderLab Group LLC
Jennifer Emmett, Erica Green, Kate Hale, *Founders*

Editor Maya Myers; **Photography Editor** Nicole DiMella; **Managing Editor** Rachel Houghton;
Designers Project Design Company; **Researcher** Michelle Harris;
Copy Editor Lori Merritt; **Indexer** Connie Binder; **Proofreader** Susan K. Hom;
Sensitivity Reader Ebonye Gussine Wilkins; **Series Reading Specialist** Dr. Jennifer Albro

First American Edition, 2024
Published in the United States by DK Publishing, a division of Penguin Random House LLC
1745 Broadway, 20th Floor, New York, NY 10019

Copyright © 2024 Dorling Kindersley Limited
24 25 26 27 10 9 8 7 6 5 4 3 2 1
001-339765-Mar/2024

All rights reserved.
Without limiting the rights under the copyright reserved above, no part of this publication may be reproduced,
stored in or introduced into a retrieval system, or transmitted, in any form, or by any means (electronic,
mechanical, photocopying, recording, or otherwise), without the prior written permission of the copyright owner.
Published in Great Britain by Dorling Kindersley Limited

A catalog record for this book is available from the Library of Congress.
HC ISBN: 978-0-7440-9426-8
PB ISBN: 978-0-7440-9425-1

DK books are available at special discounts when purchased in bulk for sales promotions, premiums, fund-raising,
or educational use. For details, contact:
DK Publishing Special Markets, 1745 Broadway, 20th Floor, New York, NY 10019
SpecialSales@dk.com

Printed and bound in China

The publisher would like to thank the following for their kind permission to reproduce their images: a=above;
c=center; b=below; l=left; r=right; t=top; b/g=background
Lillian Aberback for WonderLab Group: 18c; **Alamy Stock Photo:** Brian Overcast 30clb, PR Archive 23b, 25,
Hiram Rios 1, USFWS Photo 28b, Joel Villanueva 10–11b, Edwin Remsberg / VWPics 27bl; **Dreamstime.com:** 7826376
16–17, Arenacreative 24, Oleksandr Baranov 27br, Gabriela Bertolini 22br, Jordi Mora Igual 26, Elisa Lara 7b, 30cla,
Lavizzara 30tl, Littleny 23tr, Maya Kovacheva Photography 17bc, Natalia Zakharova 8br, Jeremias Ozoa 30bl, Andrei
Potorochin 11tr, Ari Purnomo 9t, Dan Rieck 7crb, Pedro Rivera 20–21, R. Gino Santa Maria / Shutterfree, Llc 14–15b,
Maxim Tatarinov 22bl, Vincent Giordano / Tritooth 18br, Warat42 11br, Dennis Van De Water 6; **Getty Images:**
Hola Images 9cl, Moment / Carlos Luis Camacho Photographs 19; **Getty Images / iStock:** anakin13 15cr,
Creatikon Studio 30cl, Juanmonino 8cla, ProArtWork 3, 6tl, 12br, 28–29c, 32cr, raksyBH 14cla; **Shutterstock.com:**
littlenySTOCK 4–5, Alessandro Pietri 29t, Dora Ramirez 12–13

Cover images: *Front:* **Dreamstime.com:** Basheeradesigns; **Getty Images / iStock:** DigitalVision Vectors / JakeOlimb crb,
ProArtWork bl, studiogstock cra; *Back:* **Lillian Aberback for WonderLab Group:** cra; **Shutterstock.com:** PO11 clb

All other images © Dorling Kindersley
For more information see: www.dkimages.com

www.dk.com

MIX
Paper | Supporting
responsible forestry
FSC™ C018179

This book was made with Forest
Stewardship Council™ certified
paper – one small step in DK's
commitment to a sustainable future.
Learn more at
www.dk.com/uk/information/sustainability

A Puerto Rican Childhood

Melissa H. Mwai

Contents

Waking Up

Carmen wakes up in her house in San Juan [SAN wahn]. San Juan is the capital city of Puerto Rico. Puerto Rico is an island in the Caribbean Sea.

Carmen puts on her school uniform. She is fast, like the lizard.

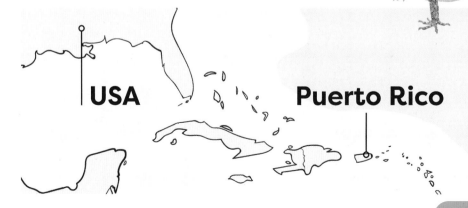

USA   Puerto Rico

Family Breakfast

Buenos días
[BWEN-nos DEE-yahs]!

Abuela [ah-BWEH-lah] is Carmen's grandma.

Carmen and her abuela eat oatmeal.

They add cinnamon.

Papi [PAH-pee] is Carmen's dad.
He drinks a cafecito
[kah-fay-SEE-toe].

Matteo is Carmen's brother. He eats the bananas from the trees in their yard.

Walking to School

Carmen and Matteo walk to school.
They spot many things.

A car zips by.
Its radio plays quick salsa music.

Hello, iguanas.
Iguanas are
big lizards.
Carmen picks up two
palm leaves and flaps
them like parrot wings.

Flap! Flap!

Class Time

Carmen is in first grade. Matteo is in seventh grade. They go to the same school.

First, Carmen has religion class. In the chapel, the class sings in Spanish and English. Today, there is no math or science. Instead, they have a field trip. Carmen is excited!

Visiting Old San Juan

Carmen's class rides the guagua [GWAH-gwah] to the neighborhood of Old San Juan.

They go to a fort called El Morro. Some of it was built in 1539. That is almost 500 years ago!

They see where soldiers ate and slept.

Carmen's favorite part of the fort is the lighthouse. This was the first place in Puerto Rico to have one.

Lunch and Kites

They eat lunch outside at El Morro. Carmen eats a jelly sandwich.
Her friend Ana shares her plantain chips. Yum!

Some kids fly kites
called chiringas
[chee-REEN-gahz].
The kites soar so high.
Carmen wants a kite, too.

**plantain
chips**

After School

After school, Carmen
goes to art club.
She draws El Morro
and kites.

Carmen plays baseball
with her friends.
Ana scores a run!
Go, Ana!

Now it is time to go home. Oh no! It is raining. Matteo runs. But Carmen jumps in puddles.

Beach Time

Later, Carmen's family goes to the beach.

Today, they visit Mar Chiquita [mahr chee-KEE-tah]. Its name means "little sea."

Carmen swims in a tide pool. The Atlantic Ocean is on the other side of the rocks. The waves are strong. Carmen swims close to her family.

Shops by the Road

Time for dinner at a kiosko [key-UHS-ko]. The cook makes food over a fire outside.

Carmen eats an empanada. The dough is crunchy and filled with meat.

empanadas

Another kiosko has a hole in the roof. Abuela says a hurricane broke it. Oh no! ¡Ay bendito! [aye behn-DEE-toh] Papi helps cover it with a tarp.

kioskos

A Phone Call

Before bed, the family calls Carmen's aunt. Tía [TEE-yah] lives in New York.

New York is a state on the mainland of the United States of America. Puerto Rico is a US territory.

Tía will visit San Juan with people from her church. They will help fix houses that are broken by hurricanes. Carmen's family will help, too.

A Blackout

The power shuts off.
This happens a lot.
There is no light.
No TV or phones.
No video games.

Matteo uses a flashlight
to make shadows.

Abuela lights candles so she can read.

What will Carmen do?

Carmen brings Papi his drum. Let's dance the bomba! [BUHM-bah] ¡Wepa! [WEY-pah]

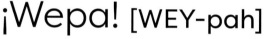

Bedtime

Carmen puts on pajamas. What's that sound? **Coqui, coqui.** There is a coquí [koh-KEE] frog under her bed.

Carmen opens the window. She lets the frog out to go live with the others.

coquí

Carmen is tired.

Good night, coquís.
Good night, mi familia
[me fah-MEEL-yah].
Good night, San Juan.

Glossary

hurricane
a storm with strong winds and heavy rain

mainland
a continent or country across the ocean from islands

tarp
a waterproof fabric covering

territory
a place that is controlled by the government of another country

tide pool
a small, protected pool at the edge of the ocean

Index

Quiz

Answer the questions to see what you have learned. Check your answers with an adult.

1. What does Carmen eat for breakfast?

2. At school, what languages does Carmen sing in?

3. What is the name of the fort in Old San Juan?

4. Which ocean is next to the tide pool in Mar Chiquita?

5. What sounds do the frogs make in Carmen's room?

1. Oatmeal 2. English and Spanish 3. El Morro
4. Atlantic Ocean 5. *Coqui, coqui*